SPECIAL OPS
Pararescuemen
in Action

by Michael Sandler

Consultant: Fred Pushies
U.S. SOF Adviser

BEARPORT
PUBLISHING

New York, New York

Credits

Cover and Title Page, © U.S. Air Force photo by Staff Sgt. Shane A. Cuomo; 4, © U.S. Air Force photo by Master Sgt. Bill Huntington; 5, © Marko Georgiev/Getty Images; 6, © U.S. Air Force photo by Master Sgt. Val Gempis; 7, © U.S. Air Force photo by Staff Sgt. Jeremy T. Lock; 8, © U.S. Air Force photo; 9, © U.S. Air Force photo; 10, © Bettmann/CORBIS; 11, © Hulton-Deutsch Collection/CORBIS; 12, © U.S. Air Force photo by Master Sgt. Val Gempis; 13, © U.S. Air Force photo by Airman 1st Class Veronica Pierce; 14, © U.S. Air Force photo by SSGT Rodney Prouty; 15, © U.S. Air Force photo by Chrissy Cuttita; 16, © U.S. Air Force photo by TSGT. Bill Thompson; 17, © U.S. Air Force photo/Master Sgt Scott Wagers; 18, © U.S. Air Force photo by Staff Sgt. Aaron Allmon II; 19, © U.S. Air Force photo by MSG David S. Nolan; 20, © NASA JSC Digital Image Collection; 21, © NASA JSC Digital Image Collection; 22, © Karl Weatherly/CORBIS; 23, © U.S. Air Force photo by TSGT John K. McDowell; 24, © U.S. Air Force photo by Staff Sgt. Manuel J. Martinez; 25, © REUTERS/David J. Phillip; 26, © REUTERS/Lee Celano; 27, © U.S. Air Force photo/Master Sgt. Kevin Gruenwald; 28TL, © U.S. Air Force photo by Senior Airman Kenny Kennemer; 28BL, © U.S. Air Force photo by SSGT David W. Richards; 28BR, © U.S. Air Force photo by SSGT Andrew Hughan; 29TL, © U.S. Air Force photo by Chrissy Cuttita; 29TR, © U.S. Air Force photo by Airman 1st Class Veronica Pierce; 29B, © U.S. Air Force photo/Master Sgt. Scott Wagers; 31, © U.S. Air Force.

Publisher: Kenn Goin
Senior Editor: Lisa Wiseman
Creative Director: Spencer Brinker
Design: Debrah Kaiser
Photo Researcher: James O'Connor

Library of Congress Cataloging-in-Publication Data

Sandler, Michael.
  Pararescuemen in action / by Michael Sandler ; consultant, Fred Pushies.
    p. cm. — (Special ops)
  Includes bibliographical references and index.
  ISBN-13: 978-1-59716-633-1 (library binding)
  ISBN-10: 1-59716-633-2 (library binding)
  1. United States. Air Force—Search and rescue operations—Juvenile literature.
2. Parachute troops—Juvenile literature. 3. Search and rescue operations—Juvenile literature. 4. Special forces (Military science)—United States—Juvenile literature. I. Title: Pararescuemen in action. II. Pushies, Fred J., 1952- III. Title.

UG633.S28 2008
358.4—dc22

                    2007034443

For more information, write to Bearport Publishing Company, Inc., 101 Fifth Avenue, Suite 6R, New York, New York 10003. Printed in the United States of America in North Mankato, MInnesota.

032011
030311CGC

10 9 8 7 6 5

Contents

After the Hurricane 4

Air Force Pararescue 6

The First Pararescuemen 8

Saving Soldiers 10

Training Begins 12

The Pipeline 14

More Training .16

A Hero in Afghanistan 18

A Space Rescue 20

An Icy Rescue .22

Saving a City .24

That Others May Live 26

The PJs' Gear 28

Glossary 30

Bibliography 31

Read More 31

Learn More Online 31

Index 32

About the Author 32

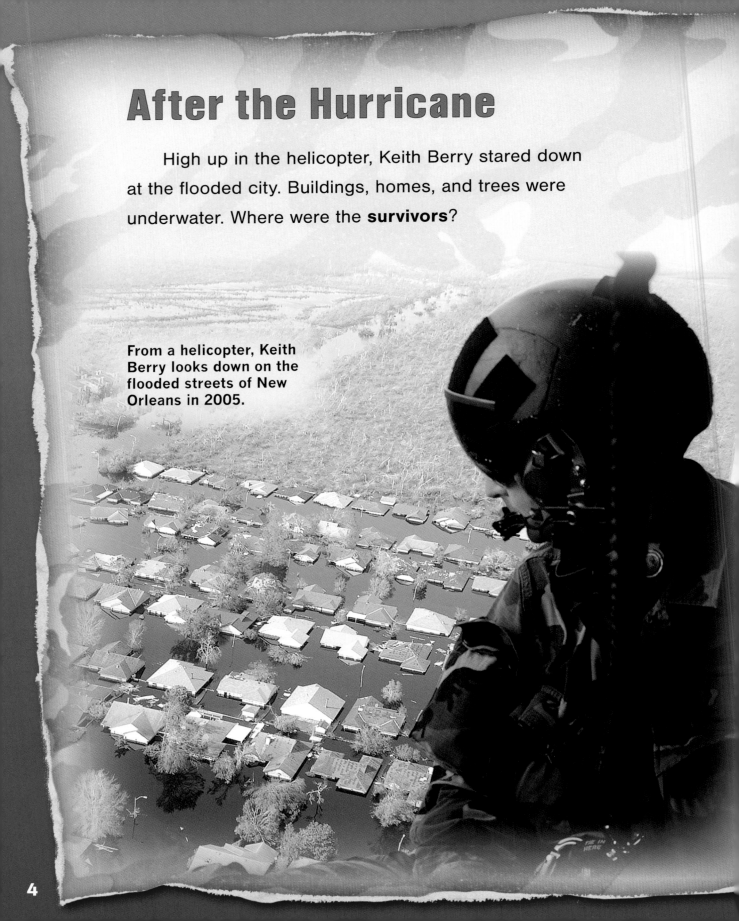

After the Hurricane

High up in the helicopter, Keith Berry stared down at the flooded city. Buildings, homes, and trees were underwater. Where were the **survivors**?

From a helicopter, Keith Berry looks down on the flooded streets of New Orleans in 2005.

Keith's eyes were tired. Like other **pararescuemen**, he'd been flying over New Orleans for hours. Suddenly, he saw something move. It was a group of people standing on a raised **median** in the flooded street. The **chopper** swung around. The crew dropped a rope out the side and Keith grabbed it. He slid down below.

Hurricane Katrina flooded New Orleans when it slammed into the city on August 29, 2005. To stay alive, people climbed onto roofs or other high places.

Air Force Pararescue

Keith Berry is a **pararescue jumper**, or a PJ. The PJs are part of the U.S. Air Force. They perform the world's toughest rescues.

Trained in medical, survival, and **combat** skills, PJs make rescues almost anywhere. They often **parachute** from planes or helicopters to get to survivors.

Only men can be PJs. It is one of only a few Air Force jobs that do not accept women.

Many of their **missions** happen during war. If a plane goes down, the PJs search for stranded **airmen**. They tend to the wounded. They may even have to fight the enemy.

PJs can parachute down 25,000 feet (7,620 m) from airplanes, jump into raging seas, and brave blizzards on the highest mountaintops.

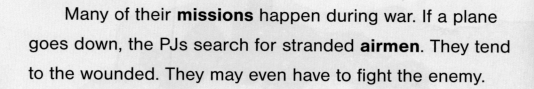 During peacetime, PJs are always ready to help out. They often make rescues during natural disasters, such as hurricanes.

The First Pararescuemen

Pararescue began in World War II (1939–1945). An Army airplane was carrying 21 Americans on a top-secret mission over Burma. Suddenly, the plane's engines failed.

Everyone parachuted out before the plane crashed. Twenty people survived the jump. However, they still weren't safe. They were deep in a jungle filled with the enemy—Japanese soldiers.

An airplane, such as this one, was carrying Americans over Burma in 1943 when it crashed.

Could they be rescued? It seemed that parachuting down to the jungle was the only way to reach the survivors. Three brave airmen were sent to rescue them. The airmen made the jump and found the survivors.

Brigadier General Donald Flickinger was one of the three rescuers.

The airmen were able to lead the survivors to safety. However, the difficult journey out of the jungle took one month. The group had to be very careful to stay away from the enemy.

Saving Soldiers

The rescue in Burma made one thing clear—pararescuemen could save lives! After World War II ended in 1945, the Air Force set up six **permanent** PJ teams.

The new teams quickly went into action during the Korean War (1950–1953). In 1950, a PJ jumped behind **enemy lines** to rescue an injured pilot in Korea. The pilot was bleeding badly.

Today, there are about 400 PJs. When not on a rescue, they wear a special maroon **beret** with their uniform.

PJs flying over Korea prepare to make a jump in March 1951

The PJ dragged him into a helicopter. The pilot was so hurt that he couldn't wait to get to a hospital for help. The PJ would have to give him medical care in the helicopter. Once in the air, the PJ began a blood **transfusion**. He saved the pilot's life.

During the Korean War, the injured were taken to hospitals such as this one aboard a U.S. ship.

Training Begins

Becoming a PJ is not easy. Jason Cunningham, a senior airman, began his two-year training in 1999. The hard work started with a 10-week course. Some call it Superman School.

Airmen may do 1,000 sit-ups a day in the mud!

Every day **trainees** wake up at 4:30 A.M. They spend the next 18 hours running, swimming, weight training, and climbing up ropes 35-feet (11-m) high. Sometimes they also have to lift huge logs or pieces of railroad track. To finish the day, trainees often march for miles wearing 50-pound (23-kg) backpacks.

The 10-week training course is one of the most difficult in the **Armed Forces**. Only the strongest men make it through the program.

Trainees have to lift very heavy logs.

The Pipeline

The PJs who pass Superman School, then head to the Pipeline. This group of courses takes about a year and a half to complete.

Training begins with parachute school. Putting all fears aside, PJs learn to jump from planes.

Airmen working together during parachute training

Next up is underwater school, where PJs become expert scuba divers. They also practice escaping from plane crashes at sea.

PJs also spend 22 weeks in **paramedic school**. They are taught to treat bullet wounds, **splint** broken bones, and perform **field surgery**.

Dive course trainees happily reach the shore.

During the Pipeline, PJs travel cross-country from one course to the next. In the mountains of New Mexico, for example, they practice climbing. On New York City streets they work with paramedics treating gunshot victims.

More Training

Another part of the Pipeline is survival school. A week in the wild teaches PJs to stay alive without supplies. No water? PJs collect **dew** that gathers each morning on their parachutes and then drink it. No food? PJs discover how tasty crunchy bugs can be!

Trainees learn fire-making techniques while in survival school.

One of the Pipeline's longest courses is combat training. In war, saving lives can mean fighting the enemy. So PJs must become experts with rifles and pistols. They learn to defend themselves in any situation.

An airman performs a search during combat training.

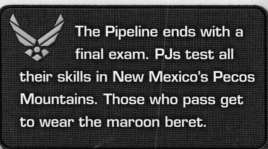

The Pipeline ends with a final exam. PJs test all their skills in New Mexico's Pecos Mountains. Those who pass get to wear the maroon beret.

A Hero in Afghanistan

In 2001, Jason Cunningham finished his PJ training. Soon he was sent to Afghanistan. There, U.S. Armed Forces were fighting the **Taliban**.

PJs have saved more than 750 lives in Afghanistan and Iraq.

Jason and his team flew over enemy land to rescue trapped soldiers. A rocket hit their helicopter. The chopper crashed to the ground.

As Taliban rockets flew by, Jason stayed by the helicopter. He helped care for the injured and carried them to safety.

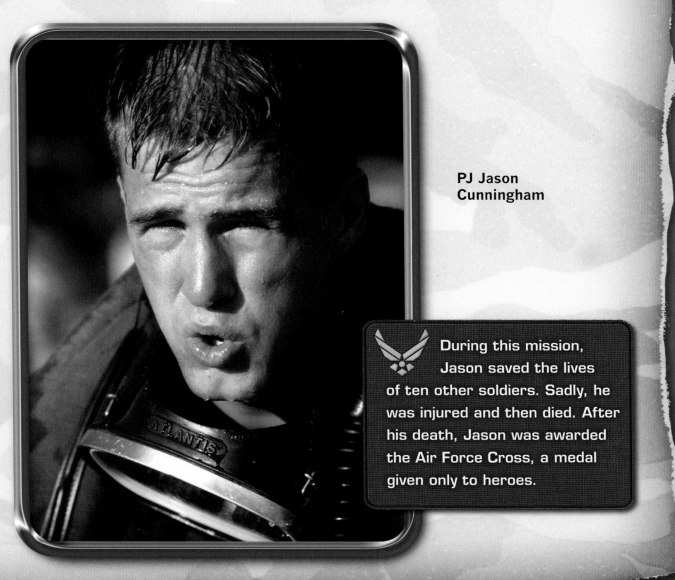

PJ Jason Cunningham

During this mission, Jason saved the lives of ten other soldiers. Sadly, he was injured and then died. After his death, Jason was awarded the Air Force Cross, a medal given only to heroes.

A Space Rescue

PJs not only have rescued other soldiers, they have even saved astronauts. In 1966, the spacecraft *Gemini 8* was in trouble. It had begun to spin out of control. The astronauts had to make an emergency return to Earth.

The spacecraft landed in the ocean. However, the rescue ships were too far away. So **NASA** called in the PJs.

Gemini 8 **launches into space.**

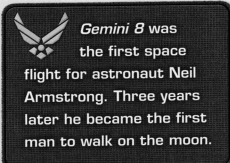

Gemini 8 was the first space flight for astronaut Neil Armstrong. Three years later he became the first man to walk on the moon.

Air Force planes zoomed toward the astronauts. Three PJs parachuted down and hooked a **floater** to the spacecraft. They kept the astronauts from sinking until the ships arrived.

Astronauts Neil Armstrong and David Scott sit in their spacecraft surrounded by three PJs.

floater

An Icy Rescue

For PJs in Alaska, saving mountain climbers is part of their job. In 2002, four men set out to climb Mount Saint Elias. Near the top, two fell and died.

Pro snowboarder John Griber was one of the two climbers who needed to be rescued. He had hoped to snowboard down the mountain.

Mount Saint Elias is the second-highest mountain in the United States. Climbing to the top of this 18,008-foot (5,489-m) mountain is very dangerous.

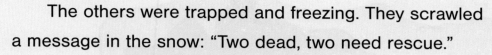

The others were trapped and freezing. They scrawled a message in the snow: "Two dead, two need rescue."

It is hard to land a helicopter on an icy mountain. However, the PJs were ready for the challenge. They flew toward the mountain and spotted the climbers. The pilot landed the chopper, which slid across the ice toward the tired men. Once the chopper came to a stop, the men climbed on board.

The pilots and PJs of Alaska's 210th Rescue Squadron saved the climbers' lives. This PJ, also from the 210th Rescue Squadron, prepares to splint a survivor's leg.

Saving a City

Hurricane Katrina hit New Orleans hard during August 2005. Hundreds of PJs like Keith Berry came to help.

PJ Lem Torres lifts a young boy to safety from the roof of a flooded home.

In the first five days after Katrina struck, PJs rescued more than 2,000 people.

When Berry spotted some survivors, he quickly dropped from the chopper onto the flooded street. One by one, he hooked people to a rope. Then he helped **hoist** them into the helicopter. When the chopper was full, it flew away.

Berry stayed behind. More survivors waited in a nearby building. He went inside and led them onto the roof. There, Berry helped load them into helicopters **hovering** above.

More survivors about to be rescued in New Orleans

That Others May Live

Luckily, disasters the size of Hurricane Katrina don't happen often. Rescues, however, always need to be made. For this reason, PJs are ready at a moment's notice. They keep training even after making the team. Each day is a chance to improve their rescue skills.

A PJ wearing his maroon beret

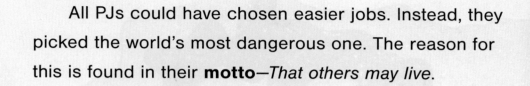

All PJs could have chosen easier jobs. Instead, they picked the world's most dangerous one. The reason for this is found in their **motto**—*That others may live*.

Most PJs spend about eight years as pararescuemen.

The PJs' Gear

PJs use lots of equipment to carry out their missions.

Here is some of the gear they use.

HH-60G Pave Hawk helicopters take PJs to and from rescue sites.

The **HALO parachute system** is used when PJs need to make rescues behind enemy lines.

PJs use **climbing gear** to make rescues on mountaintops.

Scuba equipment allows PJs to make underwater rescues.

PJs carry medical backpacks filled with about 80 pounds (36 kg) of supplies.

PJs use many types of guns during combat.

Glossary

airmen (AIR-men) soldiers who use planes or other aircraft during war

Armed Forces (ARMD FORSS-iz) the military groups a country uses to protect itself; in the United States these are the Army, the Navy, the Air Force, and the Marines

beret (buh-RAY) a round, flat hat made from a soft material

chopper (CHOP-ur) a helicopter

combat (KOM-bat) fighting

dew (DOO) the water in the air that collects on things that are outside

enemy lines (EN-uh-mee LINEZ) areas of land from where the enemy fights

field surgery (FEELD SUR-jer-ee) medical operations done outside of a hospital

floater (FLOH-tur) a device that keeps something from sinking

hoist (HOIST) to lift up using a rope

hovering (HUHV-ur-ing) flying in place without moving up, down, or side to side

median (MEE-dee-uhn) a piece of land that separates two sides of a street

missions (MISH-uhnz) special jobs

motto (MOT-oh) a saying that states what someone believes in

NASA (NAS-ah) the National Aeronautics and Space Administration; the group responsible for U.S. activities in space

parachute (PAH-ruh-*shoot*) to jump out of a plane or helicopter using a soft cloth attached to ropes to slow down the fall

paramedic school (*pah*-ruh-MED-ik SKOOL) a place where people are trained to give emergency medical treatment

pararescue jumper (*pah*-ruh-RESS-kyoo JUHMP-ur) a person who jumps out of airplanes or helicopters in order to rescue people

pararescuemen (*pah*-ruh-RESS-kyoo-men) Air Force soldiers who are trained to make rescues, give medical care, and fight in combat

permanent (PUR-muh-nuhnt) created to last forever

splint (SPLINT) to secure a person's arm or leg using a stiff object to keep broken bones from moving around

survivors (sur-VYE-vurz) people who live through an accident or disaster

Taliban (TAL-uh-*ban*) a military and political terrorist group that ruled Afghanistan from 1997 to 2001

trainees (trane-EEZ) people who are learning how to do something by practicing

transfusion (transs-FYOO-zhuhn) giving blood to an injured person

Bibliography

Drury, Bob. *The Rescue Season*. New York: Simon & Schuster (2001).

Hirsh, Michael. *None Braver: U.S. Air Force Pararescuemen in the War on Terrorism*. New York: NAL Caliber (2003).

Huntington, Master Sergeant Bill. "A PJ's Night in New Orleans." *Air Force News Service* (September 12, 2005).

McKenna, Pat. "Superman School." *Airman Magazine*, Vol. 44, Issue 2 (February 2000).

Pushies, Fred. *U.S. Air Force Special Ops*. St. Paul, MN: Zenith Press (2007).

www.af.mil/ (official site of the U.S. Air Force).

Read More

Covert, Kim. *U.S. Air Force Special Forces: Pararescue*. Mankato, MN: Capstone Press (2000).

Gonzalez, Lissette. *Search and Rescue Specialists*. New York: PowerKids Press (2007).

Visser, Reona. *Story of a Storm: A Book About Hurricane Katrina*. Brandon, MS: Quail Ridge Press (2006).

Learn More Online

To learn more about the PJs, visit
www.bearportpublishing.com/SpecialOps

Index

Afghanistan 18–19

Alaska 22–23

Armstrong, Neil 20–21

Berry, Keith 4–5, 6, 24–25

Burma 8–9, 10

Cunningham, Jason 12, 18–19

Flickinger, Brigadier General Donald 9

Gemini 8 20–21

helicopter 4–5, 6, 11, 19, 23, 25, 28

Hurricane Katrina 4–5, 24–25, 26

Iraq 18

Japanese soldiers 8

Korean War 10–11

maroon beret 10

Mount Saint Elias 22–23

New Orleans 4–5, 24–25

parachutes 6–7, 8–9, 14, 16, 21, 28

Pipeline, The 14–15, 16–17

spacecraft 20–21

Superman School 12, 14

Taliban 18–19

training 6, 12–13, 14–15, 16–17, 18, 26

U.S. Air Force 6, 10, 19

World War II 8, 10

About the Author

Michael Sandler has written many books for children and young adults. He lives in Brooklyn, New York, with fellow writer Sunita Apte and their two children, Laszlo and Asha.